Praise For

JUST LEAVES

In *Just Leaves*, Lauren Best comes to grips with words as emotional vehicles in all their mutability, a task more challenging than catching minnows with bare fingers. The process can be frightening, requiring the exposure of vulnerabilities, but Best is categorical: there must be "no story left unturned".

She also knows what counts: compassion, caring, curiosity and creativity are at the heart of her practice as a cultural worker, and she brings these to her exploration of inner states as much as to her conclusions on poetry itself. Her reckoning with the trickiness of language leads to some exciting conclusions, such as that "letters don't/make sounds/with dependable angles".

Perhaps the strongest part of the book is the section entitled *Kitchen*, which explores recipes at once as instructions to be followed and also as complex narratives in themselves, containing intricate (often bewildering) histories. Most significantly, recipes possess emergent properties: recipes are greater than the sum of their instructions, as they physically bring together disparate things - things often sourced from places that are worlds apart in time and space - to create new wholes greater than the sum of their parts.

Equally rewarding is *fire side (late watch)*, Best's extended and wide-ranging meditations during an all-night vigil. This is not a dark night of the soul, but a reckoning with the self, between the self and an unnamed addressee, and between the self and the outside world. The conclusion of this section comes with a categorical demand that could stand for the entire book's thesis: the only way to read and express the universe is through poetry.

Richard-Yves Sitoski
Owen Sound Poet Laureate
2019-2023

JUST LEAVES

JUST LEAVES

LAUREN BEST

First paperback edition June 2023

Book design by Samantha Blake (blakeedits.com)
Front cover photograph by Lauren Best
Back cover photograph by Dylan Chauvin-Smith

ISBN 978-1-7389604-0-8

Published by Lauren Best
laurenbest.com

thank you to those who read and those who listened

Preface

While writing these poems my life was jubilant and turbulent, cresting and crashing in waves of death, grief and rebirth. I transformed as I examined my identity and relationship to creativity, reckoning with my abilities, awareness, and understanding of power and poetry. I wrote glimpses into my mind, and odes to complexities.

I became poet laureate in 2017. I was a young mother and still recovering from profound loss, trauma, and change. The focus of my tenure was on children, and I served that goal as a primary responsibility, subsuming my own story. I was confronting postpartum and parenting experiences and living a life too complicated to explain with poetry.

I dutifully focused on fulfilling the laurel mission, to raise my posture to be worthy of the limited-time crown of leaves as if it was a neon halo rather than grown in dirt. I felt inspired but reeling, and it seemed almost unreal to publicly emerge with this position and confidence.

Determined to rise to the occasion, I was still piecing together difficult emotional mosaics in my personal life and untangling a new concept of self as I healed and learned. I was troubled by what I saw in my community and changing world, and wanting to make a difference while overwhelmed by possibility.

Creating the collection picked up momentum once I realized it would become a book. In some cases, I started drafts by speaking the poems into voice-to-text or recordings, because the ideas would arrive quickly and inconveniently, with no notebook or pen in sight. My role as poetic ambassador began to feel more integrated with the rest of my messy beautiful life.

Though this book is primarily intended for an adult audience, there are poems in this collection connected to young people and interwoven with community based practices. Other poems created during my tenure were more personal and reflective.

My time as poet laureate ended in 2019, while I was completing the finishing touches on the manuscript. I was optimistic that it would be published as my first full-length book by the end of 2020.

Before this poetry collection was ready to be in the hands of readers, I moved back into the house by the lake, where many of the poems began, from the one bedroom downtown apartment I shared with my preschooler. I then proceeded to survive a pandemic, be shook by death and heartbreak, get engaged, and birth my second son.

When I finished writing the poems for this book I thought the long and difficult part was over. I would have been shocked to know that I would create an entire new human being before the book would be in print.

I created a podcast, poems from this collection were published in anthologies, and I started other poetry projects. At times, I felt I'd moved beyond these poems, and I hadn't even published the collection yet.

I think it's been worth the wait. In 2018 I was galvanized by the idea of traditionally publishing this collection. Instead, I embarked on a self-publishing journey culminating in print, digital, and audio editions. I'm proud of embracing the opportunity share these poems, shining a light to discover the path that eventually navigated this specific book here to this moment, to you.

I hope that something in this book gives you a feeling of movement, a spring in your step, a breeze that awakens you. May it inspire in ways that ripple through your timeline, and reverberate to touch the lives of others.

Lauren Best
Owen Sound, 2023

Acknowledgements

Special thanks, with deep love, to my family for their unwavering support and patience.

I gratefully acknowledge the assistance of the Owen Sound & North Grey Union Public Library's stewardship of the program. I'm thankful for the legacy and collegiality of other poets laureate past and present, near and far, and for the poets and musicians not recognized by official funding or titles yet deserving laurel leaves of their own.

I am deeply indebted to the mentorship, friendship, and support that led to this collection of poetry. The feedback and encouragement I received continues to ripple through the pages and beyond me.

This was not an accident. Incredible generosity, courageous spirit, and dedication of individuals, organizations, and communities of practice that have blessed me with opportunity and acceleration. I have supporters standing behind me as ancestors and mentors, many of them poets. Generations of nurturing has led to my charmed life, my creative practices, my poems, and this book.

Many thanks to the readers and listeners who have let me know that they appreciate something I've created, and remind me to keep going. Without you, it wouldn't be quite like this. I am forever in loving gratitude.

JUST LEAVES

TABLE OF CONTENTS

OUT SIDE

wrds

words have a life of their own
they say
they travel
stray
catch before they release

I have grown to know I need them
written down
I can't remember
all of those beautiful things you said
falling through one ear
and out my other

I fear
I won't remember-
I can't write it all
though
goodness no

it feels the same as before
so-so
our memories aren't all that reliable
we play the reel back like rewind

funny how just as
you can't yourself fast forward
backwards doesn't last either

we think we've got it
clearly captured
but really it's slipping away
water
draining

(try to grab and
reverse that flow)

remembering isn't as easy as
recoloured frames
freezable and acclaimed

somehow words capture-
not the experience of writing them-
but envision
light directly
those moments
regression

past life
redirection
writing history or making it undone

leaving no story left unturned
no song left unsung

driving forward
planning
more dreams

directions
drafts
dredging themes
scoring scenes

scattering seeds
branching
repeat

(really, any direction you please)

words I can rely on more than memories

sorta scary, really-
just a few moments to make
collections of words that could
amount to more
than
most of my days

swept away
hidden or flying
floating on sound waves
fading
souring
or boring

doesn't take long to make
collaborations of characters that can
devastate
decimate
defeat or
liberate

negotiate
debate
demonstrate
initiate or
complicate

set straight
delineate
mandate and evaluate

choose, construct, calculate

when it's written
I can remember
and I can see
before my eyes

so, future self
(and other future selves)
to be honest
and true
remember:

what direction will you point your wand
and what enchantments will you utter

what seeds shall you sow
what do you intend to yield

do you nourish
or deplete the earth
that you ask to cradle you
create for you
make safe for you

make do

where do your words go?

choice

how do you use your voice?

simple. short.
clear counts.
compassion
counts.
caring counts.
curiosity
counts.
creativity counts.

it amounts

starts
sparks
fuels
reflects and remarks

little parts

we all know words are arrows
we have felt in our hearts

Poet Tree

a poem is waiting just for me
perched upon my poet tree

hidden in the wave of leaves
my poet tree grows A B Cs
L M N O canopies
cue our estimates
of words
wondering what sits
among those letters

when the leaves shudder
do metaphors drop like acorns
or whirl like maple horns

helicopter flight of fancy
potential unicorn
and rhinoceros dancing

sit and see
why the poet tree
will make you pleased
possibly smile
or sing
or wonder
or just be

look up at the poet tree

(double you:

ex?

why?)

spring dragons

early spring dragons
shadow ice dewdrops, glimmer
breath upon the sun

rustling soft spruce hands
with wingbeats as they arrive,
tired from winter

they sniff at the snow,
each exhale melting more ice
into frosted mud

spring dragons clear paths,
tails ringing white coral bells
for rabbits and ducks

count on them to leave
useful items for children
prone to adventure

sticks and supplies for
quests to discover magic
and further courage

attention in several pieces
or, Heat In Three Parts

1

my attention is damaged
imagining your voice
    i want to hear
      you whisper

I bruise, ripe and
wilting,
over
 come
   by
Distraction
 itchy and prickling
heat, and déjà vu

2

attention: fractured
seeping crude
leaks and spills

always running to the lowest point
trickling down my neck, the
path of least
resistance

3

quench
drenched

I wring my hands and wrench
    loose moments,
memorize lists
            reorganize

          i think i would like to pet a lemur

or prepare lunch

valley dusk

the sky just turned from
blushed pink to
grey violet,
and as the clouds
become more blue-

reflection sinking
into smudged storm,
ombré darkening-

I spend poetry
on you,
sticky words
like credit
that I don’t have

accumulation

sometimes I wonder
if I didn't talk so much

____

could I count the weight,
measure the volume of words
accumulating

pale dusk piled behind
squall, faint feathers whirl degrees
of separation

I sweat, warmly watch
sing sweetened vowel curves into
cold conversation

my speech sinks concave-
opposite of arc, arch, crest
lends memory _________

KITCHEN

screen capture

how can I possibly
Screen
Capture
sympathy,
heartbreak-
it doesn't add
up, the letters don't
make sounds
with dependable angles

numerals rattle with decimal
pinging, hollow
brittle
bouncing bones
making an alphabet soup,
dry noodles in a rusty can

shake, shake, shake

aching horizon wakes
and the words
still are not
sufficient
for mothers and sons,
sisters and daughters

loss is like permafrost
I slowly thaw
but keep hurtling away
from a frozen moment

when they say free fall
This is what They mean

or falling forwards, time suddenly leading
away from you instead of towards you

this is what they mean

landmarking my life line
(mines)
punctuation profound

Recipes, part 1

recipes used to be
crafted from my grandmother's caring
kitchen demonstration
learning cultivated in the creation

recipes used to be
clipped from magazines

flipped to
a slightly stained book page

photocopied, maybe
laminated occasionally

meticulously filed
fit to card
double-sided
scrawled
in blue pen cursive loops

or printed
gifted
numbered steps
measured
and left to be lifted and refitted
drifting from tradition to
... just delicious!

recipes used to be
requested
while ascending to tastes that
make any face look like heaven

exchanged and collected
connecting the connected

recipes used to be
so highly regarded
sometimes wrought with expectation
fraught with flagrant exclusion

coercively extracted from
hesitant in-laws and
guarded and guessed at

named secret and kept isolated
in the name of safe saving
of family skill trading

recipes used to be
a need

now sent digitally
scanned, typed or
simply shortened bit.ly
occasionally by text
if requiring urgency

I can google something more frugal
if the ingredient list is too brutal
combine
redesign

(I never find
quite the right
recipe for how I feel
tonight)

Recipes, part 2

recipes used to be
top secret

guarded
like some savoured cross
between a family heirloom
and military intelligence

(bake for one hour
medallions of honour-
but do these treasures
risk treason?
check your oven
for generational security-
that edges to middle
cook evenly)

recipes used to be
waged to be won

fairground flair to find
winners fair
or as a family feud
or as a friendly duel
or as a story spun

tall tales
a chance to
Really be Someone

recipes used to be
book worthy
bound hardcover
resources, listed

researched
reconnaissance recovered
revised, reprinted, rediscovered-

been read
word spread

for more to read
words worthy of folded corners
floured creases

faint stains on favoured pages
the odd drop of some slop that slipped
mid spoon dip
during a recipe consultation moment,
a short communion with the deity of
recipes

a pause and considering
of the cause

the conversions
the calories
what's thawed

a moment between a cook and a book
and then a drip
under the instructions
as if to note the reason to look

but now recipes are as seen on TV
saved with printscrn
screencap
(grab,
clip,
pin)
or top upworthy

Recipes, Part 3

recipes used to be
told and retold
in the form of stories

spun daily after dinner
cordless receiver
light on
20 minutes minimum-
sometimes an hour,
hour and a half-
even though we lived five minutes away
even though we saw each other daily

these stories
are how we
take care of each other, ladies

I want to nourish you
I want you to nourish your babies
like how I nourished
you as a baby

I want these recipes
to go to you
from me

to be reminded of this story
my improvements
this recipe's history
the ways I make it just right for me
the ways I take it
the ways I mould it

it was meant to be
for this recipe to pass from
you to me
from me to you

for all the food of my table
to somehow nourish you
through my experiments
through my modifications

through this platform for sharing
that gives us a way to be daring
even if it's not known while eaten

I know
I'll be speaking that recipe to you
after dinner
while we chat
while I settle my food

baked

today i will be like
apple crumble

delicious and nutritious
despite falling apart

warm to the touch
a bit sticky
spiced

lemon leaving you wanting
more sweetness
and crunch

BED ROOM

maybe (a blemish revealed)

I have a mosquito bite
just above my collar
bone
I discover it
and itch to show you

it feels strange to try to
take a
shoulder selfie,
and I stop
because this is ridiculous,
why would you want
to observe from afar

(when really
I want
to show you
but have you see

the focal point
created by venom
the itch rising
and standing unashamed)

weeks later,
I found raised pink
blooming circular
perched on the curve of a
rib bone
between side and back
between up and down

still, I ached
to tell you,
trace your fingers
along topographic tones

unimportant as secrets
jolting and jilted

maybe it would be a
surprise to you

it was to me, led by feel
and stretching, swiping
stroking skin awake

maybe it would have
given pause
allergic
annoyance memorialized

(perhaps it would have
given you
curiosity without
kindness

I wonder if
it is possible to know
like sticky fingerprints
what may smudge
or disarm you)

notice

sometimes I imagine
you watching me
-not in a weird
creepy way,
not like
hiding

I just want to imagine
myself as beautiful
in everyday moments
in moments every day

and I appreciate the warmth
of my cheeks
streaked with
dappled light
and drying tears

the wind lifts my
skirt to slide
swinging simply
softly astride

in a shockingly desperate
measure

I imagine you
notice

just

would it make you feel
uncomfortable
if I spoke directly to you
let longing slip

if I speak of your magnificence
and aim my poetry at your eyes

sat with you
and unpacked
how gorgeousness stirs me

and creases in your smile
make light disappear
and dawn again

would it be too much
to deadpan desire

just say the sort of
slow-simmered saucy
self-immolating burning needs
that flicker and firestorm

I want to soothe you
but also stir you
and if I can,
surprise you
sometimes

select
some parts of me
to show you

maybe you'll stick
around to see
what's next

slow learning

I want to touch you as slowly
as practice

with some space
to feel the vibrations
notice the resonance

I want to be suspended
improvising
I want cadence
and phase

I answer every question
again,
all day long

(I never have enough time
and space to expand upon)

take your wonders
seal them in bottles
send them to me

I will uncork them
and hear the escaping

sounds of being
washed ashore

like slow practice,
you challenge me

I can’t contain my thoughts
through repetition
deliberation
here I am
destination
not withstanding

the ache of attention
pushing against
patterns and
polyrhythms

like practice
I imagine more than I can do
or say

I visualize movements
with precision
ease
grace
and poise

(instead making the same mistake,
again)

lifeboat

there's no container,
no line,
no vanishing point-

a crumbled trail
for you to follow
into marrow of daydreams

to poke about
make yourself known

so there is a history of hope
when the syllables
stick their arms out,
stuck in my throat

not down or up
just dangled
over the moat

the crocodiles lunge,
snapping at their toes
but maybe we can coax them
into the lifeboat

really, it's safe!
I'll help you float!

but they're not so convinced

small spaces keep me safe,
I've learned by rote

better rudderless
than soaked

I know you'll need to find me-
I feel that with certainty

I need to have a map
I need curiosity
more than courtesy

I'm leaving a bit of space
for you to meet me in this place

give up the chase,
arrive and aerate

oh, to set a date?
it's there any time
but don't be fucking late

FIRE SIDE

fire side (late watch)

8:00 pm

Preface

a small section of my mind
has been reserved
to keep a fire lit

to park my myself there
as needed

curl up
retreat and stare

please allow me
to smoulder
wait to tell me
it's time

10:20 pm

Introduction

it's my personal fantasy, right?

you don't have to
necessarily share those

and maybe when
I tell it all, it's a bit
too on the nose,
you know?

just because you think it
don't mean you have to sing it

on the nose like
how I wish you'd
softly kiss me
and how I probably share
a bit too much
of my history

and sometimes my thoughts
(fade too much,
shrink at my touch)
do not seem enough-
but if I write it down
it feels

a little less
rough

I don't build every detail,
I leave places to be patient

lest I carelessly create
great expectations
bound blindly to fail

expecting mail,
setting paper boats to sail,
waiting for words,
tracking without a trail

I hope I shoot blanks into space
to leave incomplete

the fire
or the premise
at the centre

12:34 am

A Proposal

so I'll go back to the beginning

I'll set the scene:
there's a fire fading,
you're reading to me
or maybe we're sitting silently

perhaps I'm sprawled
or pinched tight like a pierogi
elbows poking
holes in my salty pretzel curves

I don't really care so specifically
to sort sound

I want you to know me
I want to listen
I don't need to recognize the story

nope, it won't bore me
it is the tones and tongue clicks
I'm looking for mostly

the resonance shifting
magnetic mapping oration
swaying rhythms ghostly

I want to host, see-
so I've made this moment of
flame and now,
maybe I'm merely boasting

but it's not to compete-
batches of bait
laid out before I sleep

seek sweet
dream in shadow
and relief

sculpting landmarks
so we can find
one another
when it's time
to meet

I make checkpoints
in my mind
while I check out-
points of prayer so I know
what I'm really about

dropping down
dangled up
over the moat

measuring distance
between mud
and soap

I was hoping
to make a little,
manageable moment

but I got carried away
in what I thought were
careful currents

imagining the texture of your lungs

2:45 am

Lament

however, no one notices
if it's Fire Place:
The Hallowe'en Edition

it's only me editing the
conditions of this rendition

just one curator
one narrator
so I can wonder what we'd read
and equate atmosphere

consider creativity of creatures
or rather revelations of fear

say, from the shelf:

the Signet Classic
Mary Shelley's
Frankenstein

wrapped in softcover,
small serif living
agreeably alongside
Dracula,
Dr. Jekyll,
and Mr. Hyde

would you open it
without mark and start to read?

would you speak syllables so slowly
turn pages into poetry

I don't need them all in order
we can read backwards
stumble on exposed roots of
pathetic fallacy

just open
your mouth
and sing
windy songs
to me

the cover shows a red sky-
is that supposed to be foreboding?
but
what about
sailor's delight?
(call the publisher people,
this isn't right)

y'know, I got this book
back in high school-
the cover had a corner
torn off
kinda like it got in a fight

and dog eared
got more scrappy

soft card stock
bent with creases
buckled veins
tattered
rounded edges
fraying feathered

honestly, it looks like a thick book-
three friends deep in defence-
but it still bows
turns a cheek
to accidental slights,
to displays of might

anyway, the cover got ripped
so my English Literature teacher-
otherwise a sensible
and book loving individual-
told me to
throw
it
out

... really?

yeah, just recycle it.

that seemed really wrong,
not only one but three stories
made to fly in the world:
gone.

if I kept it,
worst case it could be
paper airplanes,
best case,
a song

erasure-
mostly for poetry.

oh, because most importantly:
we had only studied the Shelley

just one book out of three!
ya took a three fer one
and forgot to take the deal

(I know sir, there's only
so much in just one semester
that can be adequately studied)

anyway, I was
seventeen and
I once
called Huck Finn
ingenious
in a final exam essay

(squeezing options
from cramped hands)
when the word I was looking for
had no innovation,
in fact it seemed placating-
but despite my reach
in marker on
the foolscap sheet
it was explained to me
that resourceful is what I meant

... uh, like not judging by softcover?

peek under those
scratched wings,
laminated luminous,
softened with
beatings,
bent

posts a sign but
it doesn't pay the rent

so- you can imagine
the glee with which
I had to rescue this book
from certain death

because even though it seems
like just the right thing to do,
it was a helluva steal-
a free book! actually,
not just one
but an extra two

can I keep it?

sure.

well there it is,
10 plus years,
how many moves later?

still on my shelf
mottled music to be played

and if I'm being honest
stacked in
a taller grave

4:01 am

Clarification

if I curled up
with a fire fading,
my head in your lap
                like a cat
-yes definitely
like a cat-
is monster madness
what you'd read to me?
    only on hallowe'en?

I don't mind
if you choose,
that one just sprung
to mind since it
had been rescued,
packed and unpacked,
honestly sort of neglected
and after such abuse
(a tale that isn't new
for lonely paperbacks
leased to quick
cohorts of youth)
    I could leave the
Hallowe'en Edition
of the fire
for next year

no rush-
I would still be curled up
well into November

I wonder if
you could build columns around me
hang mosquito netting

your voice drifting,
smokey and strong into
newsprint rafters

your fingers smudging
the leftover sap of
words onto my cheek

okay, I admit:
I thought it didn't
have to be quite so scary
just for hallowe'en

I would have listened
to the news too
from you
in that fantasy

it drifted
into my planning,
my vying-
but current events are
fucking terrifying!

just in case anyone
had not been
paying attention

(which I do understand-
it's hard to hear,
partial to worming
into the heart
from the ear
whether you catch it
on the tv at the bank
or just a
quick mention)

last breath,
extended credits
scroll by
rolling time uphill

taut from toe
to testicle

surely should be
primary concern

but we return
coming around the
life of the cycle

reasonable to be critical
it's not that insightful
excuse me for finding it
more frightful
than viral mutation
at it's most basic

no politics,
religion or
science, delightful

I may appear
to be losing composure
but don't mistake
my disclosure
for an overture
in fact,
perhaps I'm seeking
closure

            you could just
read me the local news

they qualified for provincials?
            but barely before
the closing of their school

it's okay, I'll be soothed
by fundraising updates
on page two

well, there's the gap
that they are trying to pack
with crochet Christmas ornaments
and hats with ear flaps,
to build a bridge to
better public services
with legion dances
and 50/50 purses

stop the leak with
peanut butter
marshmallow squares
stuck in the holes-
tax receipts
available for donations
equal or greater to
emerald queen (the second)

the bill is made from plastic,
it won't soak up the water
match volume to dollars
but maybe we can patch it
over the dripping
so that we have something for backup
once the marshmallows
meet their melting

dear maker of the fantasies
within my mind:
perhaps the news shouldn't be
part of your design

4:42 am

Closure

I place myself
quietly in the burning

you can be there too,
lower my lids from flame to ash
and try to let a soundtrack
drift into view

I hear it in the distance
but curatorial decisions are
Really
Stressful-
yes, even for
my own personal
Beside the Fire
holiday special

take a seat
the relaxation
is in the retreat

it's not about the destination
obviously
arriving and wondering
is enough for me

so music can
swing surrounding
sneak up like surprise

don’t know when the smoke
will start to sting your eyes

I know, I’m imaging it
the responsibility is on me

but I like leaving a space
a wait and see

I thought I might ask
you to choose
because really,
I don’t care what
it is you are saying

whether you
talk about
nothing or
raise significant silence

yawn, roar,
retch,
rustle and
stall to read

it's your voice in the dark
it's the smell of combustion
the protesting wet bark

I would be better
to shut up
for once

what will be
will be,
what we'll read
will read

so please
speak to me
say anything

just let it
be
poetry

Manufactured by Amazon.ca
Bolton, ON

34331952R00055